THE PULL OF THE CULT

UNDERSTANDING THE PSYCHOLOGY BEHIND BELIEF

ARAVINDH

Copyright © Aravindh
All Rights Reserved.

This book has been self-published with all reasonable efforts taken to make the material error-free by the author. No part of this book shall be used, reproduced in any manner whatsoever without written permission from the author, except in the case of brief quotations embodied in critical articles and reviews.

The Author of this book is solely responsible and liable for its content including but not limited to the views, representations, descriptions, statements, information, opinions and references ["Content"]. The Content of this book shall not constitute or be construed or deemed to reflect the opinion or expression of the Publisher or Editor. Neither the Publisher nor Editor endorse or approve the Content of this book or guarantee the reliability, accuracy or completeness of the Content published herein and do not make any representations or warranties of any kind, express or implied, including but not limited to the implied warranties of merchantability, fitness for a particular purpose. The Publisher and Editor shall not be liable whatsoever for any errors, omissions, whether such errors or omissions result from negligence, accident, or any other cause or claims for loss or damages of any kind, including without limitation, indirect or consequential loss or damage arising out of use, inability to use, or about the reliability, accuracy or sufficiency of the information contained in this book.

Made with ♥ on the Notion Press Platform
www.notionpress.com

INDEX

Introduction

Brief overview of cults and their characteristics

The recent rise of cults and their appeal to modern society

The purpose of the book

Chapter 1: Understanding Cults

Defining what a cult is and what sets them apart from other groups

The different types of cults and their ideologies

Historical examples of cults and their impact on society

Chapter 2: The Psychology of Belief

The human need for meaning and purpose

The role of cognitive dissonance in belief formation

The impact of emotional manipulation and the power of suggestion

Chapter 3: Factors Contributing to Vulnerability

The impact of social isolation and loneliness

The role of personal crisis and vulnerability

The impact of charismatic leaders and group dynamics

Chapter 4: Leaving the Cult

The psychological impact of leaving a cult

The challenges of reintegrating into society

The role of support and therapy in the recovery process

Some specific benefits of support and therapy in the recovery process include:

Conclusion

Recap of the main ideas of the book

Introduction:

Brief overview of cults and their characteristics

Cults are often characterized as groups or organizations that exhibit a high level of control over their members and have a strong influence on their thoughts and behavior. Some of the key characteristics of cults include:

Charismatic leadership: Cults are often led by a charismatic and authoritarian figure who has a strong influence on their followers. The leader is usually seen as having special powers or abilities, and members may be encouraged to place their faith in the leader above all else.

Isolation and control: Cults often exert a high degree of control over their members, including limiting contact with the outside world, controlling information, and dictating daily routines and behavior.

Belief in a unique ideology: Cults typically have a unique set of beliefs or doctrines that are often seen as absolute truths. Members are expected to accept and follow these beliefs without question.

Use of mind control and manipulation: Cults often use mind control techniques such as hypnosis, group pressure, and other forms of manipulation to influence their members' thoughts and behavior.

Financial exploitation: Some cults require members to make significant financial contributions or give up their possessions in order to demonstrate their commitment to the group.

Endorsement of extreme or dangerous behavior: Some cults may endorse or engage in extreme or dangerous behavior, such as self-harm, suicide, or violence.

It's important to note that not all groups or organizations that exhibit one or more of these characteristics are necessarily cults. However, the presence of several of these characteristics, particularly when taken to an extreme, can be a warning sign of a potentially dangerous group or organization.

The recent rise of cults and their appeal to modern society

Increased social isolation: In an age of social media and digital communication, people are more connected than ever before, but they are also increasingly isolated. Many people are seeking a sense of community and belonging, which can make them vulnerable to the appeal of a tight-knit group like a cult.

Uncertainty and anxiety: In an era of rapid change and uncertainty, people are looking for answers and stability. Cults often offer a clear, simple set of beliefs and a sense of security and purpose, which can be attractive to people who feel lost or adrift.

Disenchantment with traditional religion: Some people are disillusioned with traditional religions, which they may see as outdated or out of touch. Cults can offer an alternative that seems more relevant and modern, but which can also be more extreme or dangerous.

The influence of charismatic leaders: Charismatic leaders can be very persuasive, and the rise of social media and other forms of digital communication has made it easier for them to reach and recruit followers.

The search for meaning and purpose: Many people are looking for something deeper and more meaningful in their lives, and cults can offer a sense of purpose and direction that is often lacking in modern society.

Overall, the appeal of cults to modern society is complex and multifaceted, and it can be difficult to pinpoint any one factor as the root cause. However, by understanding the reasons why people are drawn to cults, we can work to prevent their rise and protect vulnerable individuals from their harmful effects.

The purpose of the book:

The purpose of the book would be to provide a comprehensive examination of the psychology behind why people are drawn to cults and the factors that contribute to their vulnerability. The book would explore the various theories and perspectives on this topic, drawing on research from psychology, sociology, and other relevant disciplines. The ultimate goal of the book would be to increase awareness and understanding of the complex and multifaceted nature of cults and their appeal, and to provide readers with practical strategies for identifying and avoiding cults, as well as supporting individuals who may have been affected by them.

The book would be aimed at a general audience, as well as mental health professionals, religious leaders, and anyone else who may come into contact with individuals who are vulnerable to cults. It would draw on a range of real-world examples and case studies to illustrate key concepts and provide practical insights into the psychology of cults and the factors that contribute to their appeal. By providing readers with a deep understanding of the psychology of cults, the book would empower them to make informed decisions and take steps to protect themselves and others from the dangers of cults.

Chapter 1: Understanding Cults

Defining what a cult is and what sets them apart from other groups

However, some experts and researchers have identified certain characteristics that tend to be associated with cults, which set them apart from other types of groups. Here are some potential defining features of cults:

Authoritarian leadership: Cults are typically led by an authoritarian figure who has a high degree of control over their followers. This leader is often seen as having special powers or abilities, and may be revered as a messianic figure.

Isolation from the outside world: Cults often encourage or require their members to isolate themselves from the outside world, either physically or psychologically. This can include limiting contact with family and friends, controlling access to information, and requiring members to follow a strict set of rules and routines.

Manipulation and mind control: Cults often use various techniques to manipulate and control their members, including hypnosis, thought reform, and other forms of psychological manipulation.

Belief in a unique ideology: Cults typically espouse a unique set of beliefs or doctrines that are often seen as absolute truths. Members are expected to accept and follow these beliefs without question.

Financial exploitation: Some cults require members to make significant financial contributions or give up their possessions in order to demonstrate their commitment to the group.

Endorsement of extreme or dangerous behavior: Some cults may endorse or engage in extreme or dangerous behavior, such as self-harm, suicide, or violence.

It's important to note that not all groups or organizations that exhibit one or more of these characteristics are necessarily cults. However, the presence of several of these characteristics, particularly when taken to an extreme, can be a warning sign of a potentially dangerous group or organization.

The different types of cults and their ideologies

Cults can take many different forms and espouse a wide range of ideologies. Here are some potential examples of different types of cults and their beliefs:

Religious cults: These are cults that have a religious focus, often with a charismatic leader who claims to have a special relationship with God or divine forces. Religious cults may have unique and idiosyncratic beliefs that are not shared by mainstream religious groups. Examples of religious cults include the People's Temple (Jonestown) led by Jim Jones and the Branch Davidians led by David Koresh.

New Age and self-help cults: These cults tend to have a focus on personal development, self-improvement, and spirituality. They may promote unconventional or unproven health practices, like alternative medicine, meditation, or spiritual healing. Examples of new age cults include The Fellowship of Friends and The Kashi Ashram.

Political cults: These are cults that promote a political ideology or cause, and may have a charismatic leader who claims to have the solution to political problems. Political cults often involve extremist or radical ideologies, and may promote violence or other forms of illegal activity. Examples of political cults include the Bhagwan Shree Rajneesh's community in Oregon and the Aum Shinrikyo cult in Japan.

Commercial cults: These are cults that are focused on making money and may use aggressive sales tactics or pyramid schemes to recruit and retain members. Examples include Amway and Scientology.

Psychotherapy cults: These cults may offer psychotherapy or other forms of counseling, but may use coercive techniques or demand high fees for their services. Examples include the NXIVM cult led by Keith Raniere.

It's important to note that these are just some potential examples, and cults can take many other forms and have many different ideologies. However, all cults tend to share certain characteristics, such as the ones mentioned in my previous response, and may be harmful to their members and society as a whole.

Historical examples of cults and their impact on society

There have been many cults throughout history, some of which have had a significant impact on society. Here are a few examples:

The Manson Family: This was a cult led by Charles Manson in the 1960s, which was responsible for a series of gruesome murders. Manson and his followers believed in a race war, and they committed these murders in an attempt to incite it. The Manson Family had a significant impact on American culture, and the killings have been the subject of numerous books, films, and other media.

The People's Temple: This was a religious cult led by Jim Jones, which is most famously known for the mass suicide/murder of over 900 of its members in Guyana in 1978. The cult had a significant impact on American society at the time, and the tragedy remains one of the most horrific events in U.S. history.

Aum Shinrikyo: This was a Japanese cult led by Shoko Asahara, which was responsible for a deadly sarin gas attack on the Tokyo subway in 1995. The cult's ideology was a mix of Eastern and Western religions, and it had a significant impact on Japanese society, leading to changes in the country's laws regarding religion and other issues.

Heaven's Gate: This was a cult led by Marshall Applewhite, which believed that Earth was going to be "recycled" and that the only way to survive was to leave the planet on a spaceship. In 1997, Applewhite and 38 of his followers committed suicide in an attempt to reach the spaceship. The cult's impact on society was less significant than some of the others on this list, but the event was widely covered in the media at the time.

The Branch Davidians: This was a religious cult led by David Koresh, which was involved in a lengthy standoff with law enforcement in Waco, Texas in 1993. The standoff ended in a deadly fire, which killed 76 people, including Koresh and many of his followers. The incident had a significant impact on American culture, and it led to debates about government overreach and the rights of religious minorities.

These are just a few examples of cults that have had a significant impact on society, but there are many others as well. Cults can be dangerous and harmful, both to their members and to society as a whole, and it's important to understand their nature and how to identify and avoid them.

Chapter 2: The Psychology of Belief

The human need for meaning and purpose

The human need for meaning and purpose is a fundamental aspect of our psychology. At its core, this need reflects a desire to find significance and understanding in the world around us, and to connect with something larger than ourselves.

Research has shown that having a sense of purpose is associated with a range of positive outcomes, including better physical and mental health, greater life satisfaction, and a stronger sense of well-being. People who feel like their lives have meaning and purpose are more likely to be resilient in the face of stress and adversity, and they may have greater motivation and focus in pursuing their goals.

There are many factors that contribute to our need for meaning and purpose. For example, our sense of purpose may be influenced by our cultural or religious beliefs, our personal values and goals, our relationships with others, and our experiences of achievement and success.

However, it's important to note that the search for meaning and purpose can also be a source of stress and anxiety, particularly when we feel like we haven't found a clear direction or when we experience setbacks or failures. In some cases, this search can lead people to turn to cults or other harmful groups as a way of finding meaning and belonging.

Overall, the need for meaning and purpose is an important and complex aspect of human psychology, and it's one that continues to be the subject of ongoing research and exploration. By understanding this need, we can better appreciate the challenges that people face in trying to find purpose and fulfillment in their lives, and we can work to support them in this quest in healthy and positive ways.

The role of cognitive dissonance in belief formation

Cognitive dissonance is a psychological concept that refers to the mental discomfort that arises when a person holds two or more conflicting beliefs, values, or attitudes. It can also occur when a person's behavior is inconsistent with their beliefs, values, or attitudes.

In the context of belief formation, cognitive dissonance can play a significant role in shaping how people come to believe certain things. When a person encounters information or experiences that conflict with their existing beliefs, they may experience cognitive dissonance, which can be uncomfortable or even distressing. In response, they may try to resolve this discomfort by changing their beliefs or attitudes to be more consistent with the new information or experiences.

For example, let's say a person strongly believes that climate change is a hoax, but then they read a scientific report that presents strong evidence to the contrary. This new information may create cognitive dissonance, as it conflicts with their existing belief. To resolve this discomfort, they may either reject the new information and continue to believe that climate change is a hoax, or they may accept the new information and revise their belief to be more consistent with the evidence.

However, cognitive dissonance can also work in the opposite direction. For example, when people invest significant time, money, or energy in a particular belief or ideology, they may be more resistant to changing their minds, even when presented with evidence to the contrary. This is known as the "backfire effect," and it can actually strengthen a person's existing beliefs in the face of contradictory evidence.

Overall, cognitive dissonance is an important concept in understanding how people form beliefs and attitudes, and how they respond to new information and experiences that challenge those beliefs. It highlights the importance of being open-minded and flexible in our thinking, and being willing to revise our beliefs and attitudes when presented with new evidence or experiences.

The impact of emotional manipulation and the power of suggestion

Emotional manipulation and the power of suggestion can have a significant impact on a person's beliefs, attitudes, and behavior. Emotional manipulation involves using emotional appeals or techniques to influence a person's thoughts or actions, often by exploiting their fears, insecurities, or desires. The power of suggestion involves making a subtle or indirect suggestion that can influence a person's beliefs or behavior without them realizing it.

These techniques can be used by individuals, groups, or organizations to influence people in a variety of ways, such as convincing them to adopt a particular belief or ideology, convincing them to buy a product, or convincing them to support a particular cause or political candidate.

Emotional manipulation and the power of suggestion can be particularly effective when used in conjunction with other psychological tactics, such as creating a sense of urgency, using social proof or peer pressure, or appealing to authority or expertise.

For example, a cult leader may use emotional manipulation and the power of suggestion to convince their followers to give up their possessions, cut off contact with family and friends, or even engage in illegal activities. They may use tactics such as love bombing, where they shower their followers with affection and attention, or gaslighting, where they manipulate their followers into doubting their own perceptions of reality.

Similarly, advertisers may use emotional manipulation and the power of suggestion to convince people to buy their products. They may use techniques such as creating a sense of scarcity, playing on people's fears or desires, or using celebrity endorsements or testimonials to make their products seem more desirable.

Overall, emotional manipulation and the power of suggestion can be powerful tools for influencing people's beliefs and behavior. It's important to be aware of these tactics and to approach any claims or appeals with a healthy degree of skepticism and critical thinking.

Chapter 3: Factors Contributing to Vulnerability

The impact of social isolation and loneliness

Social isolation and loneliness can have a significant impact on a person's physical and mental health. Social isolation refers to the absence or lack of social contact and relationships with others, while loneliness refers to the subjective feeling of being alone or disconnected from others, even when surrounded by people.

Research has shown that social isolation and loneliness can increase the risk of a variety of health problems, including depression, anxiety, cognitive decline, cardiovascular disease, and even early death. Social isolation and loneliness have also been associated with decreased immune function, which can increase the risk of infections and other health problems.

One reason for the negative impact of social isolation and loneliness on health may be that social support can provide a buffer against stress and help people cope with difficult situations. When people lack social support, they may be more vulnerable to the negative effects of stress, which can increase the risk of developing physical and mental health problems.

Additionally, social isolation and loneliness can also impact a person's quality of life, leading to feelings of boredom, purposelessness, and lack of motivation.

The role of personal crisis and vulnerability

Personal crisis and vulnerability can have a significant impact on an individual's life and well-being. These experiences can shape a person's beliefs, values, and behaviors, and can influence their interactions with others.

In some cases, personal crises can be catalysts for personal growth and transformation. For example, a person who experiences a major life change, such as the death of a loved one, may be forced to reevaluate their priorities and make positive changes in their life.

Similarly, a person who faces a significant challenge, such as a serious illness, may become more resilient and gain a greater appreciation for life.

However, personal crises can also have negative effects. They can lead to feelings of depression, anxiety, and hopelessness. In some cases, they can even trigger mental health issues such as post-traumatic stress disorder (PTSD).

Vulnerability is another factor that can influence how people respond to personal crises. Some people are more resilient and able to cope with challenging situations, while others may struggle more. Factors such as a person's social support network, self-esteem, and previous life experiences can all play a role in how they respond to crisis.

Overall, personal crises and vulnerability can have a profound impact on an individual's life. While these experiences can be difficult, they can also be opportunities for personal growth and development. It is important for individuals to seek support when they are facing challenging situations, whether from friends and family or from mental health professionals.

The impact of charismatic leaders and group dynamics

Charismatic leaders and group dynamics can have a significant impact on individuals and organizations. Charismatic leaders are those who have an ability to inspire and motivate others through their vision, personality, and communication style. Group dynamics refer to the ways in which individuals interact with one another within a group or organization.

When a charismatic leader emerges, they can have a powerful impact on group dynamics. They can inspire members to work towards a shared goal, and can create a sense of loyalty and commitment within the group. Charismatic leaders are often seen as role models, and their behavior can be emulated by group members.

However, the impact of charismatic leaders and group dynamics is not always positive. Charismatic leaders can be authoritarian and may discourage dissent or alternative viewpoints. Group dynamics can create pressure to conform to the norms of the group, which can stifle creativity and innovation.

In some cases, group dynamics can lead to groupthink, where the desire for group consensus overrides critical thinking and decision-making. This can be particularly problematic in situations where important decisions need to be made.

Overall, the impact of charismatic leaders and group dynamics is complex and multifaceted. While they can have a positive impact on individuals and organizations, they can also create challenges and potential pitfalls. It is important for individuals to be aware of the potential influence of charismatic leaders and group dynamics, and to be vigilant about maintaining independent thought and critical thinking. Effective communication, collaboration, and the encouragement of diversity of thought can help to mitigate the negative impact of group dynamics and maximize the positive effects of charismatic leadership.

Chapter 4: Leaving the Cult

The psychological impact of leaving a cult

Leaving a cult can be an incredibly challenging and traumatic experience for individuals. Cults often use a range of psychological techniques to control and manipulate their members, including isolation, thought reform, and emotional manipulation. As a result, leaving a cult can have significant psychological impacts, including:

Emotional distress: Individuals who leave a cult may experience a range of emotions, including grief, anger, confusion, and guilt. They may struggle to come to terms with the time they have lost, the relationships that have been severed, and the beliefs that they held.

Cognitive dissonance: Leaving a cult can create cognitive dissonance, where a person's beliefs and values no longer align with their experiences or reality. This can create a sense of confusion and uncertainty, as individuals struggle to reconcile their former beliefs with the world outside the cult.

Post-Traumatic Stress Disorder (PTSD): Some individuals who leave a cult may experience symptoms of PTSD, such as anxiety, flashbacks, and hypervigilance. These symptoms can be triggered by reminders of their time in the cult, or by experiences that are reminiscent of the control and manipulation they experienced.

Loss of identity: Individuals who leave a cult may struggle with a loss of identity, as they attempt to rediscover who they are outside of the cult. Cults often encourage members to reject their former identity and to conform to the group identity, which can make the process of rediscovery challenging.

Difficulty with relationships: Individuals who leave a cult may struggle to form relationships with those outside the cult. Cults often discourage members from forming close relationships with people outside the group, and as a result, individuals who leave may have difficulty trusting others or forming connections.

Overall, leaving a cult can have significant psychological impacts, and individuals may require support and counseling as they work to process their experiences and rebuild their lives. It is important for individuals who have left a cult to seek out support from mental health professionals, as well as from support groups or loved ones who can offer understanding and empathy.

The challenges of reintegrating into society

Reintegrating into society after an extended period of separation, such as leaving a cult, being incarcerated, or experiencing homelessness, can be incredibly challenging. Some of the major challenges that individuals may face when reintegrating into society include:

Social isolation: Individuals who have been separated from society for an extended period may struggle to reestablish social connections. They may feel disconnected or ostracized, and may struggle to find a sense of belonging.

Stigma and discrimination: Individuals who have experienced incarceration, homelessness, or other forms of separation may face stigma and discrimination when they attempt to reintegrate into society. They may be viewed as dangerous, unreliable, or untrustworthy, which can create additional barriers to reentry.

Financial instability: Individuals who have been separated from society may have difficulty finding employment, securing stable housing, or accessing basic resources such as food and healthcare. Financial instability can create additional stress and can make it difficult to rebuild a stable life.

Mental health challenges: Individuals who have experienced extended separation from society may struggle with mental health challenges such as depression, anxiety, or PTSD. These challenges can make it difficult to reestablish social connections, find employment, or cope with daily life.

Lack of skills or education: Individuals who have been separated from society may lack the skills or education necessary to compete in today's job market. This can make it difficult to find employment, which can create additional financial and social challenges.

Overall, reintegrating into society can be an incredibly challenging process. It requires a great deal of resilience, perseverance, and support. It is important for individuals who are attempting to reintegrate to seek out support from loved ones, community organizations, and mental health professionals. Additionally, programs that offer job training, education, and other forms of support can be incredibly beneficial in helping individuals to rebuild their lives and find a sense of purpose and belonging.

The role of support and therapy in the recovery process

Support and therapy can play a critical role in the recovery process for individuals who have experienced trauma, abuse, addiction, or other challenges. These forms of support can help individuals to process their experiences, develop coping strategies, and build resilience.

Support can come in many forms, including family and friends, support groups, and community organizations. Having a supportive network of individuals who understand and empathize with one's experiences can be incredibly validating and healing. Support can also offer practical assistance, such as helping with job searches, providing transportation, or offering childcare.

Therapy, whether individual or group-based, can also be an important part of the recovery process. Therapists can help individuals to explore and process their experiences in a safe and supportive environment. They can provide guidance and tools for managing emotions, identifying and changing negative thought patterns, and building coping strategies. Therapy can also help individuals to develop a deeper understanding of themselves and their relationships, which can facilitate personal growth and self-acceptance.

Some specific benefits of support and therapy in the recovery process include

Validation and normalization of experiences: Talking with others who have experienced similar challenges can help individuals to feel less alone and more understood. This can help to reduce feelings of shame and isolation, and can facilitate a sense of connection and belonging.

Emotional regulation: Therapists can teach individuals techniques for managing emotions, such as mindfulness, deep breathing, or progressive muscle relaxation. These techniques can be especially helpful for individuals who struggle with anxiety, depression, or trauma-related symptoms.

Building healthy relationships: Support and therapy can help individuals to develop healthier relationships with others, by teaching communication skills, boundary-setting, and conflict resolution.

Developing self-compassion: Support and therapy can help individuals to develop a greater sense of self-compassion and self-acceptance. This can help to counteract feelings of shame or self-blame, and can facilitate personal growth and self-actualization.

Overall, support and therapy can play a critical role in the recovery process for individuals who have experienced trauma, abuse, addiction, or other challenges. They can help individuals to process their experiences, develop coping strategies, and build resilience, which can facilitate healing and growth.

Conclusion:

Recap of the main ideas of the book

A call to action to raise awareness about the dangers of cults and the need for support for those affected by them.

The main idea of raising awareness about the dangers of cults and the need for support for those affected by them is to inform the public about the potential risks of involvement in a cult and to provide resources for individuals who may have been impacted by a cult. The following are some key ideas that are often discussed in the context of raising awareness about cults:

Definition of cults: Cults are often characterized by high levels of control, isolation from mainstream society, and the use of coercive persuasion techniques. They often have a charismatic leader who claims to have special knowledge or abilities.

Risks of cult involvement: Individuals who become involved in a cult may experience a range of negative consequences, including financial exploitation, emotional manipulation, and even physical harm. Cults may also cause individuals to become isolated from their families, friends, and support networks.

Signs of cult involvement: It can be challenging to identify whether someone is involved in a cult, as they may be highly secretive or defensive about their involvement. However, there are some warning signs to look out for, such as changes in behavior or personality, sudden isolation from loved ones, and a preoccupation with a particular group or leader.

Support for those affected by cults: It is essential to provide support and resources for individuals who have been impacted by cults. This can include access to mental health services, support groups, and legal assistance. It is also important to provide education and awareness about cults to help prevent others from becoming involved.

Overall, the main idea of raising awareness about the dangers of cults and the need for support for those affected by them is to provide resources and education to help individuals avoid or recover from cult involvement. By shining a light on the risks and warning signs of cult involvement, we can work to prevent harm and support those who have been impacted by these groups.

Contents

www.ingramcontent.com/pod-product-compliance
Lightning Source LLC
LaVergne TN
LVHW010445070526
838199LV00066B/6198